THE YOGA SUTRAS OF PATANJALI

संस्कृतम्
PUBLICATION

THE YOGA SUTRAS OF PATANJALI

Illustrations, Introductions, Book Summary, & Translation

by: संस्कृतम् Publication
Original Sanskrit Text/Author: Patanjali
Publication Year: 2024
Publisher: संस्कृतम् Publication

First Edition

INTRODUCTION

The Yoga Sutras of Patanjali is one of the most important and revered texts in the tradition of yoga philosophy. Attributed to the sage Patanjali, this ancient work provides a thorough and structured guide for understanding the principles and practices of yoga. Comprised of 196 concise aphorisms, the sutras outline a clear path to spiritual freedom and self-realization.

Patanjali's Yoga Sutras offer a roadmap for individuals seeking to understand themselves, presenting wisdom on the workings of the mind, the barriers to spiritual progress, and techniques for overcoming these challenges to achieve deep inner peace and enlightenment. The text is divided into four chapters, or "padas," each exploring different dimensions of yoga philosophy.

Samadhi Pada: This first chapter introduces the concept of Samadhi, a state of deep meditation and unity with the divine. It explains how focused attention and mental clarity lead to inner stillness, laying the foundation for all other practices in yoga.

Sadhana Pada: The second chapter delves into the practical path of spiritual discipline. Patanjali outlines the practices of Kriya Yoga, as well as the Eightfold Path (Ashtanga Yoga), which includes ethical observances, physical postures, breath control, and meditation. This chapter emphasizes the importance of consistent practice and self-discipline.

Vibhuti Pada: In this chapter, Patanjali describes the powers and insights that can be attained through advanced yogic practices. These include heightened concentration, clarity, and intuitive knowledge.

Kaivalya Pada: The final chapter focuses on the ultimate goal of yoga—liberation or Kaivalya. Patanjali explains the nature of spiritual freedom, where the practitioner transcends the limitations of the mind and experiences pure consciousness, free from attachment and suffering.

CONTENTS

1 SAMADHI PADA (BOOK ON CONTEMPLATION)

INTRODUCTION TO BOOK 1

Book 1 of The Yoga Sutras of Patanjali, known as Samadhi Pada, lays the foundational framework for understanding the path of yoga. The term "Samadhi" refers to the state of profound concentration, mental stillness, and spiritual absorption, while "Pada" translates to "chapter" or "section." This chapter focuses on the theory and practice required to still the mind and achieve self-realization.

Patanjali begins by defining yoga not just as a physical or mental practice but as the cessation of the mind's modifications or fluctuations. The aim is to quiet the restless mind so that the true self, or "seer," can emerge in its pure form. When these mental disturbances are removed, the practitioner experiences their true nature, free from external influences and misidentifications.

The chapter introduces essential concepts such as the five types of mental modifications, which include correct knowledge, misconception, verbal delusion, sleep, and memory. Patanjali also provides the tools needed to control these modifications: practice (abhyasa) and detachment (vairagya). Through persistent practice and the cultivation of non-attachment, the mind can move towards higher states of concentration, culminating in the experience of Samadhi.

Samadhi Pada outlines various obstacles that arise on the yogic path, such as laziness, doubt, and sensory distractions. However, Patanjali offers practical methods to overcome these challenges, including breath control, meditation on positive virtues, and focusing on a chosen object of concentration. The ultimate goal is to reach a state of pure awareness, where the mind becomes like a clear crystal, reflecting only the true nature of the self without interference.

This chapter emphasizes both the philosophical underpinnings and the practical aspects of yoga, making it a guide for seekers who aim to attain mental clarity, inner peace, and spiritual awakening. Through discipline, meditation, and a deep commitment to the path, practitioners can achieve Samadhi—a state of unity and complete absorption in the self, where all mental turbulence ceases and enlightenment is realized.

BOOK 1

1.1 Now, the exposition of yoga begins.
The first sutra marks the beginning of the instruction on yoga. It indicates a readiness for deeper knowledge, suggesting that the student has already prepared through prior learning or practice. "Atha" (now) signifies the commencement of a disciplined path toward self-realization.

1.2 Yoga is the cessation of the modifications of the mind.
This definition of yoga is profound. Patanjali explains that yoga is not merely physical postures or breathing exercises but the complete stilling of the mind's movements (vrittis). The mental fluctuations—thoughts, emotions, and reactions—are what bind us to an illusory experience of life. Through yoga, we quiet these fluctuations, allowing the mind to become clear and steady.

1.3 Then, the seer abides in their true form.
When the mind is no longer disturbed by distractions, the individual can experience their true nature. This sutra teaches that our essential self is ever-present, but it is obscured by the noise of the mind. In the quiet of mental stillness, the seer—the pure consciousness—can rest in its original state, free from external identifications.

1.4 At other times, the seer is identified with the mental modifications.
When the mind is active and unrestrained, we confuse ourselves with our thoughts, emotions, and external experiences. We mistakenly identify with the temporary modifications of the mind, losing sight of our true, changeless self. This leads to attachment, suffering, and ignorance.

1.5 The mental modifications are fivefold and are either painful or painless.
Patanjali introduces five kinds of mental modifications (vrittis). These modifications can either lead to suffering or be neutral. Understanding these categories helps the practitioner recognize how the mind operates and what types of modifications are beneficial or harmful to spiritual progress.

1.6 They are correct knowledge, misconception, verbal delusion, sleep, and memory.
The five types of mental modifications are outlined:
- Correct knowledge (pramana) is knowledge gained through direct perception, inference, and testimony.
- Misconception (viparyaya) is false understanding based on incorrect perception.
- Verbal delusion (vikalpa) is imagining something that is not real, often based on words or concepts without corresponding reality.
- Sleep (nidra) is a state of mental modification where there is no conscious awareness, but the mind still functions.
- Memory (smriti) is the retention of past experiences, which can shape our present reality.

1.7 Correct knowledge is based on direct perception, inference, and scriptural testimony.
True knowledge is categorized into three sources:
- Direct perception (pratyaksha) is immediate knowledge gained through the senses.
- Inference (anumana) involves logical deduction based on known facts.
- Scriptural testimony (agama) refers to knowledge received from authoritative sources, such as scriptures or enlightened teachers.
These are the valid means by which the mind can gain accurate knowledge of the world.

1.8 Misconception is false knowledge, not based on the real form of the object.
Misconception arises when we interpret or perceive things incorrectly. This false knowledge leads to confusion and suffering. For example, mistaking a rope for a snake would cause unnecessary fear and anxiety. Misconception distorts our reality.

1.9 Verbal delusion is knowledge based on words devoid of a corresponding reality.

Verbal delusion occurs when we are deceived by language or concepts that have no grounding in reality. This type of mental modification is purely abstract, and while it may seem logical, it doesn't reflect the truth. For instance, believing in a fantastical creature because of a story, even though no such creature exists in reality, is an example of verbal delusion.

1.10 Sleep is a mental modification that has the sense of nothingness as its content.

Even in deep sleep, where there is no conscious thought, the mind continues to operate. In this state, the content of the mind is the experience of "nothingness," and while restful, sleep is still a form of mental modification. Yoga seeks to go beyond even the unconscious mind.

1.11 Memory is the retention of previously experienced objects.

Memory shapes our current perception by recalling past experiences. While memory can be helpful, it can also be a source of distortion if past experiences influence us in ways that limit our perception of the present. Yoga encourages detachment from memory to stay present and avoid biases.

1.12 These mental modifications are restrained by practice and detachment.

The two keys to mastering the mind are practice (abhyasa) and detachment (vairagya). Consistent practice develops discipline, while detachment reduces our attachment to worldly desires. Together, they create the foundation for a peaceful, focused mind.

1.13 Practice is the effort to stay firmly in that state.

Practice is not just physical exercise; it is a steady, intentional effort to remain in a state of mental stillness and self-awareness. This effort must be continuous to be effective.

1.14 It becomes firmly grounded when practiced for a long time, without interruption, and with reverence.
True mastery requires sustained effort over an extended period. Patanjali emphasizes that practice must be consistent, uninterrupted, and carried out with dedication and devotion. Only then does it become deeply rooted in one's life.

1.15 Detachment is the consciousness of having mastery over desire for the seen and the unseen.
Detachment is the ability to remain unaffected by desires for material or spiritual gain. It involves recognizing that both worldly pleasures and spiritual attainments are temporary and do not lead to lasting fulfillment. Through detachment, the practitioner transcends desires.

1.16 The higher form of detachment arises from the knowledge of the true self, where the qualities of nature no longer influence the mind.
As the practitioner deepens their understanding of the self, they become free from the influence of the three gunas (qualities of nature). This detachment leads to liberation, where the mind is no longer swayed by external forces, and the individual abides in their true nature.

1.17 Samprajnata Samadhi is attained through meditation on gross objects, subtle objects, joy, or the sense of "I-am-ness."
Samprajnata Samadhi refers to the state of complete absorption where the mind is still aware of an object. It progresses through four stages:
- Meditation on gross objects (vitarka) relates to the physical world and tangible objects.
- Meditation on subtle objects (vicara) involves concepts or abstract ideas.
- Joy (ananda) is the bliss experienced in deep states of meditation.
- The sense of "I-am-ness" (asmita) is the meditative state where only the pure sense of self remains.

In this state, the practitioner experiences the essence of objects or ideas without interference from the mind.

1.18 The other type of Samadhi, asamprajnata, is attained through the practice of cessation, leaving only the latent impressions.
Asamprajnata Samadhi is a higher state of absorption where the mind is completely free from any object of focus. The impressions or samskaras (mental imprints) are still present but inactive. This state is characterized by a deep inner stillness, and it can lead to liberation from the cycle of birth and death.

1.19 Those who attain the highest form of non-attachment merge into nature or the formless state.
Patanjali describes certain beings who, through their spiritual development in previous lifetimes, have already achieved a high level of detachment and do not need further effort to attain liberation. They merge into prakriti (nature) or dissolve into a formless, enlightened state.

1.20 Others follow the path through faith, energy, mindfulness, concentration, and wisdom.
For those who have not yet attained the highest state of detachment, Patanjali outlines a practical path. This path involves:
- Faith (shraddha): Belief in the path and the process of yoga.
- Energy (virya): The effort and enthusiasm required to sustain practice.
- Mindfulness (smriti): Constant awareness of the present moment.
- Concentration (samadhi): Deep focus on the object of meditation.
- Wisdom (prajna): The clear knowledge that arises from sustained practice and understanding.

1.21 For those with intense dedication, Samadhi is near.
The intensity of one's dedication determines how quickly they can attain Samadhi. Those who practice yoga with great fervor and commitment reach the goal faster than those with a moderate or mild effort.

1.22 There are different levels of intensity: mild, moderate, or intense.
Patanjali acknowledges that practitioners approach yoga with varying levels of intensity. The more intense the dedication and effort, the quicker the results. However, all levels of practice, when pursued with sincerity, lead to progress on the path.

1.23 By devotion to God, Samadhi can also be attained.
In addition to personal effort, Patanjali presents devotion to Ishvara (God or a supreme being) as another means of attaining Samadhi. This path involves surrendering to a higher power, trusting that divine grace will lead to liberation.

1.24 God is a special purusha, untouched by afflictions, actions, and the results of actions.
Unlike individual souls (purushas), who are bound by karma and the results of their actions, God is beyond these limitations. God is free from afflictions (kleshas) and unaffected by the law of cause and effect.

1.25 In Him lies the seed of omniscience.
God is the source of all knowledge and wisdom. The seed of omniscience resides in God, making Him the ultimate teacher for all beings.

1.26 He is the teacher of even the ancients, unbound by time.
God, being eternal, has been the guide and teacher of even the ancient sages. God's wisdom transcends time and is available to all seekers, regardless of when or where they exist.

1.27 His expression is the sacred sound of Om.
The sacred syllable "Om" is considered the vibrational manifestation of God. It represents the primal sound of creation and the ultimate reality. Chanting Om and meditating on its meaning helps the practitioner align with the divine.

1.28 Repeating Om and meditating upon its meaning leads to the realization of God.
By chanting Om with focus and meditating on its significance, the practitioner purifies the mind and moves closer to self-realization. This practice helps overcome mental distractions and leads to spiritual insight.

1.29 Through this practice, the obstacles to self-realization and the distractions of the mind are removed.
Regular practice of chanting Om and meditating on its meaning gradually dissolves the mental obstacles (antarayas) that prevent spiritual progress. This leads to clarity of mind and steadiness in practice.

1.30 These obstacles include disease, dullness, doubt, carelessness, laziness, sensuality, false perception, failure to reach firm ground, and instability.
Patanjali lists specific obstacles that disrupt the practice of yoga. These obstacles arise from the mind and body and can hinder concentration and progress. Overcoming these requires consistent effort and dedication.

1.31 Accompanying these distractions are pain, depression, unsteadiness of the body, and disturbed breathing.
When the obstacles take hold, they lead to additional challenges like physical discomfort, mental distress, lack of control over the body, and irregular breathing. These symptoms further disturb the mind and make meditation difficult.

1.32 To counter these obstacles, practice single-pointedness.
The remedy for overcoming obstacles is one-pointed concentration (ekatattva). Focusing the mind on a single object or idea with unwavering attention helps quiet distractions and brings stability to the practice.

1.33 The mind is calmed by cultivating friendliness toward the happy, compassion for the suffering, delight in the virtuous, and indifference toward the wicked.

Patanjali offers a simple and powerful method to calm the mind:

- Be friendly toward those who are happy.
- Be compassionate to those who are suffering.
- Feel joy in the presence of virtuous people.
- Maintain equanimity and detachment toward those who behave wickedly.

By adopting these attitudes, we can maintain inner peace and avoid mental disturbances caused by emotional reactions.

1.34 Or, the mind is calmed by regulating the breath.

Another technique to calm the mind is through breath control (pranayama). Slow, deep, and rhythmic breathing helps stabilize the mind and body, reducing stress and anxiety. This practice also prepares the mind for deeper states of meditation.

1.35 Or, one can focus on an inner sense of light or radiance.

Focusing the mind on an inner light or sensation of radiance can also bring stability and peace. This visualization directs the mind inward, promoting clarity and concentration.

1.36 Or, meditate on a peaceful mind that is free from sorrow.

Reflecting on a state of mind that is calm and free from pain or suffering helps bring about mental tranquility. This practice aligns the mind with positive and peaceful thoughts.

1.37 Or, focus the mind on a spiritually evolved person who is free from attachment.

By contemplating a spiritually advanced individual or a saint who is detached from worldly desires, the practitioner can emulate their qualities and move closer to a peaceful mind.

1.38 Or, contemplate the knowledge gained in dreams or deep sleep.
In deep sleep or in certain types of dreams, the mind experiences a state free from distractions. Meditating on this pure state helps the practitioner understand the deeper workings of the mind and brings clarity.

1.39 Or, meditate on any object of choice that helps bring stability to the mind.
Patanjali acknowledges that different people may find different methods effective. He suggests meditating on any object or concept that resonates with the practitioner and helps steady the mind.

1.40 The mind can be trained to focus on the smallest or the largest objects.
The mind has the capacity to focus on the most minute details or the grandest concepts. Through practice, one learns to master the mind's ability to concentrate on any scale of object, whether subtle or gross.

1.41 When the mind is free from distractions, it becomes like a crystal, reflecting the knower, the object of knowledge, and the process of knowing equally.
When the mind reaches a state of pure concentration, it becomes transparent, like a crystal. In this state, the mind clearly reflects the object of meditation, the one meditating, and the process of meditation itself, without any distortion.

1.42 When the mind engages in deliberation, the samadhi is called savitarka, involving words, their meaning, and conceptual understanding.
Savitarka Samadhi is a state of meditative absorption where the mind is still engaged with thoughts and concepts related to the object of meditation. There is a deliberation between the word, its meaning, and the knowledge it conveys.

1.43 When the memory is purified, and the mind remains focused only on the object itself, without the interference of words or concepts, the samadhi is called nirvitarka.

Nirvitarka Samadhi is a deeper state of absorption where the mind no longer deliberates or engages in conceptual thought. The practitioner's awareness is solely focused on the object itself, without words or mental commentary.

1.44 In the same way, savichara and nirvichara refer to meditations on subtle objects.
Similar to savitarka and nirvitarka, these two terms refer to meditation on more subtle objects. Savichara involves deliberation on these subtle objects, while nirvichara transcends deliberation, focusing solely on the object's essence.

1.45 The state of subtlety continues until one reaches the most subtle level, which is unmanifest.
Meditation on subtle objects can continue until the practitioner reaches the most subtle form, which is unmanifest and beyond the physical senses. This state transcends all forms and enters the realm of pure consciousness.

1.46 These states of samadhi are associated with a seed that supports the state of meditation.
These stages of samadhi are called "sabija" or "with seed," meaning there is still some form of support (the object of meditation). While profound, these states are not yet the ultimate realization, as they depend on an external focus.

1.47 When the nirvichara samadhi is attained, there is clarity and spiritual illumination.
In the state of nirvichara samadhi, the mind becomes crystal-clear, free from all distractions. This clarity leads to spiritual illumination, where the practitioner experiences deep wisdom and insight.

1.48 In this state of clarity, the knowledge attained is filled with truth.
The wisdom or knowledge (prajna) gained in this state of clarity is direct and free from error. It is a pure, unmediated understanding of the truth, unlike knowledge gained through the senses or intellect.

1.49 This knowledge is different from that which is gained through study or inference, as it is direct and unmediated.
The knowledge gained in this state of samadhi is beyond ordinary intellectual understanding. It is an intuitive realization that surpasses knowledge obtained through study, reasoning, or testimony.

1.50 This type of knowledge leaves an impression that prevents the formation of other mental impressions.
The knowledge attained in samadhi creates a profound impression (samskara) on the mind, which prevents the formation of other, lower impressions. This impression guides the practitioner toward liberation.

1.51 When even this impression is removed, seedless samadhi is attained, and all mental modifications are completely restrained.
The final state of samadhi is "nirbija" or "seedless." In this state, there are no mental modifications or impressions left. The mind is completely still, and the practitioner experiences ultimate liberation.

BOOK 1 SUMMARY

Samadhi Pada introduces yoga as a practice for calming the mind and attaining spiritual awareness. Patanjali defines yoga as the cessation of mental fluctuations, where the mind becomes still and peaceful. This stillness is achieved through dedicated practice and detachment from desires.

The chapter outlines obstacles like ignorance, ego, and fear, which disrupt mental clarity. Patanjali offers solutions through meditation, mindfulness, and surrender to Ishvara, the supreme consciousness.

Two types of Samadhi are described:

·Samprajnata Samadhi: Meditation with awareness of the object.

·Asamprajnata Samadhi: Deeper meditation without awareness of any object.

Samadhi Pada sets the foundation for using yoga to quiet the mind and reach enlightenment.

2 SADHANA PADA (BOOK ON PRACTICE)

INTRODUCTION TO BOOK 2

Book 2 of The Yoga Sutras of Patanjali, known as Sadhana Pada, outlines the practical steps and disciplines necessary to progress on the path of yoga. The term "Sadhana" means practice or discipline, and this chapter serves as a guide for anyone seeking to purify their mind, body, and soul in pursuit of self-realization. Unlike the first chapter, which focuses on the theoretical aspects of yoga, Sadhana Pada offers a clear, methodical approach for practitioners to overcome the obstacles that hinder spiritual growth.

The chapter introduces Kriya Yoga, a path of action that consists of three essential practices: tapas (austerity), svadhyaya (self-study), and Ishvara pranidhana (surrender to God). These practices help weaken the mental afflictions, known as kleshas, which are the root cause of human suffering. Patanjali identifies the five main afflictions: ignorance, egoism, attachment, aversion, and fear of death. These afflictions cloud the mind and prevent the practitioner from realizing their true nature.

Central to this chapter is the introduction of the eight limbs of yoga, or Ashtanga Yoga. This comprehensive framework includes ethical guidelines (yama and niyama), physical postures (asana), breath control (pranayama), sense withdrawal (pratyahara), concentration (dharana), meditation (dhyana), and ultimate absorption (samadhi). These limbs serve as the foundation for purifying the body and mind, enabling the practitioner to progress toward spiritual liberation.

Sadhana Pada emphasizes that yoga is not merely a physical or intellectual pursuit; it is a way of life that integrates moral, mental, and physical discipline. By following the prescribed practices with dedication, the practitioner can reduce the influence of the kleshas, quiet the fluctuations of the mind, and ultimately achieve freedom from suffering. This chapter is a practical roadmap for anyone seeking transformation and self-realization through yoga.

BOOK 2

2.1 Tapas (austerity), Svadhyaya (self-study), and Ishvara Pranidhana (devotion to God) form the practice of Kriya Yoga.

The practice of Kriya Yoga, which is a subset of Patanjali's system, involves three elements:

- Tapas is the disciplined effort to purify the body and mind. This could include practices like fasting, breath control, or mental discipline, which generate inner heat to remove impurities.
- Svadhyaya refers to self-study, particularly the study of sacred texts and the reflection on one's own thoughts and actions.
- Ishvara Pranidhana means surrendering to a higher power. It encourages the practitioner to offer the fruits of their actions to God, relinquishing attachment to the outcomes.

Together, these practices form Kriya Yoga, which helps to control the fluctuations of the mind and leads to self-mastery.

2.2 This practice is undertaken for cultivating Samadhi and for weakening the afflictions.

The purpose of Kriya Yoga is twofold:

- To cultivate Samadhi, the deep state of concentration where the mind becomes still.
- To weaken the kleshas or afflictions, which are the root causes of suffering. By reducing the influence of the kleshas, the practitioner moves closer to the goal of liberation (moksha).

2.3 The afflictions are ignorance, egoism, attachment, aversion, and clinging to life.

Patanjali identifies five primary afflictions, known as kleshas:

- Avidya (ignorance): The root cause of all suffering, which leads to misconceptions about the nature of reality.
- Asmita (egoism): The false identification of the self with the mind, body, or personality.
- Raga (attachment): Desire for pleasurable experiences, leading to cravings and attachment.
- Dvesha (aversion): Aversion to pain, which leads to fear, avoidance, and suffering.
- Abhinivesha (clinging to life): The fear of death and a deep-rooted attachment to one's physical existence. These kleshas create mental disturbances and prevent the mind from attaining clarity.

2.4 Ignorance is the field for the others, whether they are dormant, weak, intercepted, or active.

Ignorance (avidya) is the foundation upon which the other afflictions rest. Without ignorance, egoism, attachment, aversion, and clinging to life would not exist. The other kleshas can exist in four states:

- Dormant: Hidden, waiting for the right conditions to arise.
- Weak: Present but not powerful enough to influence behavior.
- Intercepted: Temporarily suppressed or controlled but not eliminated.
- Active: Fully manifest and influencing thoughts, emotions, and actions.

2.5 Ignorance is seeing the non-eternal, impure, painful, and non-self as eternal, pure, pleasant, and self.
Ignorance causes a fundamental misperception of reality. It leads us to see the transient world as permanent, the impure as pure, suffering as pleasure, and the non-self (such as the body or mind) as the true self. This mistaken understanding is the root of all suffering.

2.6 Egoism is the identification of the power of the seer with that of the instrument of seeing.
Asmita, or egoism, is the false identification of the seer (the true self) with the mind and senses (the instruments of perception). When we believe that our thoughts, emotions, and physical body define who we are, we become trapped in a limited understanding of self.

2.7 Attachment is the clinging to pleasure.
Raga, or attachment, arises from the desire to repeat pleasurable experiences. This craving creates mental disturbances, as the mind becomes focused on seeking pleasure and avoiding anything that threatens its sense of happiness.

2.8 Aversion is the clinging to pain.
Dvesha, or aversion, is the flip side of attachment. It is the desire to avoid pain and suffering. This avoidance often leads to fear, anxiety, and rejection of unpleasant experiences, further disturbing the mind.

2.9 Clinging to life, flowing by its own force, exists even in the wise.
Abhinivesha, the fear of death, is a deeply ingrained survival instinct. Even the most enlightened beings experience this clinging to life, as it operates at a subconscious level. However, through practice, this fear can be transcended.

2.10 The subtle forms of these afflictions are to be eliminated by resolving them back into their cause.
The subtle forms of the kleshas are those that lie dormant or weak. These must be eliminated by tracing them back to their root cause—ignorance. Through deep meditation and inner reflection, the practitioner can dissolve these subtle afflictions.

2.11 Their active forms are to be eliminated by meditation.
When the afflictions become active, they must be dealt with through meditation. By focusing the mind and observing the mental fluctuations without attachment, the practitioner can weaken and eventually eliminate the kleshas.

2.12 The repository of karma, rooted in the afflictions, brings experiences in the present life or in future births.
The kleshas give rise to karma, which is stored as impressions (samskaras) in the mind. These impressions influence future experiences, whether in this life or in future incarnations. The cycle of karma continues until the afflictions are completely eradicated.

2.13 As long as the root exists, it will bear fruits in the form of birth, life span, and experiences of pleasure and pain.
As long as the kleshas persist, they will continue to generate karma, resulting in rebirth, the duration of life, and the experiences of pleasure and pain. The only way to break free from this cycle is to eliminate the kleshas at their root.

2.14 These experiences result in pleasure or pain, depending on whether the actions are virtuous or non-virtuous.
The experiences we encounter—whether pleasurable or painful—are the direct result of our past actions. Virtuous actions lead to pleasure, while non-virtuous actions result in pain.

2.15 To the discerning person, all is painful because of the pains caused by change, anxiety, latent impressions, and the conflict among the qualities of nature.
To the wise and discerning person, even pleasure is ultimately seen as a source of pain. This is because pleasure is fleeting, subject to change, and often followed by anxiety and desire for more. The interplay of the qualities of nature (gunas) further contributes to the instability and suffering of life.

2.16 Pain that has not yet come can be avoided.
While past and present suffering may be inevitable, future suffering can be prevented by eliminating the causes of pain (the kleshas and karma). Through diligent practice, the yogi can free themselves from the cycle of suffering.

2.17 The cause of that which is to be avoided is the union of the seer and the seen.
The root cause of suffering is the mistaken identification of the seer (the true self) with the seen (the external world, including the body and mind). This false union leads to attachment, desire, and suffering.

2.18 The seen is of the nature of brightness, activity, and inertia, consisting of the elements and the senses. It exists for the purpose of providing experience and liberation.
The external world is composed of the three gunas: sattva (brightness/purity), rajas (activity/passion), and tamas (inertia/darkness). These qualities shape all matter and sensory experiences. The purpose of the seen world is to provide the soul with experiences that lead to growth and ultimately to liberation.

2.19 The states of the seen are: the specific, the non-specific, the indeterminate, and the unmanifest.
The "seen," which refers to the external world, exists in different states of manifestation:
- Specific (Vishesha): The tangible, material world, including all objects that we perceive through our senses.
- Non-specific (Avishesha): The more subtle aspects of nature, such as the atoms and energy that underlie the physical world.
- Indeterminate (Linga-matra): The subtlest forms of matter, such as the potential energy of the elements that have not yet manifested into physical form.
- Unmanifest (Alinga): The primal, unmanifest state of nature (prakriti), from which all creation arises. These different levels represent the various stages through which matter evolves, from the subtlest to the most material form.

2.20 The seer is pure consciousness, though it appears to see through the mind.
The seer, or purusha, is the pure consciousness within each individual. It is not inherently tied to the mind or body but perceives the world through the mind and senses. The mind acts as an instrument, like a lens, through which the seer experiences reality. However, the seer remains untouched and unchanged by these experiences.

2.21 The seen exists only for the seer.
The external world exists for the purpose of providing experiences to the seer. These experiences serve two purposes: to provide enjoyment and, more importantly, to facilitate liberation. The seer uses the world as a means to understand its own nature and eventually transcend it.

2.22 Though the seen ceases to exist for one who has attained liberation, it continues to exist for others because it is common to all.
For a liberated individual, the seen world no longer holds personal significance, as they have realized their true nature and are no longer attached to the material world. However, the world continues to exist for others who are still bound by ignorance and attachments. The external world is shared by all beings, even if it has lost its meaning for the liberated soul.

2.23 The union of the seer and the seen is for the purpose of the seer realizing its true nature.
The interaction between the seer (consciousness) and the seen (the material world) exists to allow the seer to experience, learn, and ultimately realize its true nature. This union is necessary for the evolution of the soul, but once the seer has understood its true identity, this union dissolves.

2.24 The cause of this union is ignorance.
The union of the seer and the seen, which causes attachment and suffering, is rooted in ignorance (avidya). It is only through ignorance that the seer identifies with the body, mind, and external world, mistakenly believing these to be its true self.

2.25 When ignorance is removed, the union ceases, and liberation (Kaivalya) is attained, which is the seer's true state.
Once ignorance is eradicated, the false identification of the seer with the seen ends, and the seer realizes its pure, unchanging nature. This is the state of Kaivalya, or liberation, where the seer is free from all attachments, desires, and sufferings. In this state, the individual is no longer bound by the cycles of karma and reincarnation.

2.26 Discriminative knowledge is the means to liberation.
The practice of viveka (discriminative knowledge) is the key to attaining liberation. Discriminative knowledge involves the ability to discern between the real (the seer) and the unreal (the seen). By continuously practicing this awareness, the practitioner gradually loosens their attachment to the material world and moves toward liberation.

2.27 This knowledge progresses through seven stages, leading to the highest knowledge.
Discriminative knowledge unfolds in stages, becoming progressively clearer as the practitioner deepens their understanding of the self and the world. Patanjali indicates that there are seven stages in this process, culminating in the ultimate realization of the seer's true nature, free from the bonds of ignorance and attachment.

2.28 By the practice of the limbs of yoga, impurities are destroyed, and discriminative knowledge shines forth, leading to liberation.
The regular practice of yoga's eight limbs cleanses the mind and body of impurities (both physical and mental). As these impurities dissolve, the light of discriminative knowledge shines more clearly. This knowledge ultimately leads to freedom from suffering and the realization of one's true self.

2.29 The eight limbs of yoga are: yama (moral restraints), niyama (observances), asana (posture), pranayama (breath control), pratyahara (withdrawal of the senses), dharana (concentration), dhyana (meditation), and samadhi (absorption).
Patanjali introduces the eight-limbed path of yoga, known as Ashtanga Yoga, as the method for attaining liberation. Each limb is a step on the path toward mental clarity and spiritual realization:
- Yama: Ethical principles or moral restraints.
- Niyama: Personal observances or disciplines.
- Asana: The practice of physical postures to steady the body and mind.
- Pranayama: Control and regulation of the breath to purify the mind and body.
- Pratyahara: Withdrawal of the senses from external objects to focus inward.
- Dharana: Concentration on a single object or thought.
- Dhyana: Meditation, a continuous flow of concentration on a single object.
- Samadhi: Complete absorption, where the practitioner merges with the object of meditation, leading to the state of oneness with the self.

2.30 The yamas are non-violence, truthfulness, non-stealing, chastity, and non-possessiveness.
The yamas are the first limb of yoga and represent ethical guidelines for interacting with the external world:
- Ahimsa (non-violence): Practicing compassion and avoiding harm to others in thought, word, and deed.
- Satya (truthfulness): Commitment to honesty in all aspects of life.
- Asteya (non-stealing): Refraining from taking what is not freely given.
- Brahmacharya (chastity or moderation): Maintaining control over one's physical and mental energy, particularly in relation to desires.
- Aparigraha (non-possessiveness): Letting go of material attachments and the desire to accumulate wealth or possessions.

2.31 These yamas are universal, not limited by class, place, time, or circumstances, and constitute the great vow.
Patanjali emphasizes that the yamas are universal principles, applicable to all people, regardless of social status, geographic location, time, or situation. These ethical restraints form the foundation of the yogic path and should be followed consistently by every practitioner.

2.32 The niyamas are purity, contentment, austerity, self-study, and devotion to God.
The niyamas are the second limb of yoga and represent personal disciplines or observances that help cultivate inner purity and mental clarity:
- Shaucha (purity): Maintaining cleanliness of both body and mind.
- Santosha (contentment): Practicing acceptance and gratitude for what one has, regardless of external circumstances.
- Tapas (austerity): Developing self-discipline through practices that generate inner heat to purify the body and mind.
- Svadhyaya (self-study): Reflecting on one's thoughts, actions, and the study of sacred texts to gain deeper insight into the self.
- Ishvara Pranidhana (devotion to God): Surrendering to a higher power and recognizing that ultimate control lies beyond the ego.

2.33 When disturbed by negative thoughts, opposite ones should be cultivated.
Patanjali offers a practical method for overcoming negative thoughts: cultivate the opposite. If one is overcome by anger, practice compassion; if one feels greed, practice generosity. This mental discipline helps to purify the mind and redirect it toward positivity and clarity.

2.34 Negative thoughts such as violence, whether done, caused, or approved, and arising from greed, anger, or delusion, cause endless suffering and ignorance. Thus, cultivating opposite thoughts is essential.
Violent or negative thoughts, whether actively carried out, encouraged in others, or even silently condoned, all lead to suffering and further ignorance. These actions stem from greed, anger, and delusion, and perpetuate the cycle of suffering. Practicing positive thoughts and actions counters these negative tendencies and purifies the mind.

2.35 When non-violence is established, hostility ceases in its presence.
When a person fully embraces ahimsa (non-violence), their very presence creates an atmosphere of peace, where hostility and aggression naturally dissipate. Others around them instinctively feel calm and non-threatening, as the practitioner radiates compassion and non-violence.

2.36 When truthfulness is firmly established, actions and their results are rooted in truth.
By firmly practicing satya (truthfulness), the practitioner aligns with the deeper truths of existence. As a result, all actions and their outcomes are rooted in honesty and integrity. This creates a harmonious relationship between the individual and the world around them, leading to clarity and trust.

2.37 When non-stealing is established, all jewels come to the yogi.
When a practitioner firmly adheres to asteya (non-stealing), it creates an inner state of abundance and contentment. They no longer crave what others possess, and as a result, opportunities, wealth, and resources seem to come naturally into their life. This doesn't imply material riches alone but also refers to the richness of experience, wisdom, and fulfillment.

2.38 By steadfastness in chastity, energy is gained.
Brahmacharya (chastity or control over desires) leads to the conservation of energy. When one practices moderation and control over physical, mental, and emotional desires, that conserved energy is redirected toward higher spiritual goals. This energy manifests as vitality, mental clarity, and a deeper capacity for concentration in yogic practice.

2.39 When non-possessiveness is established, knowledge of past lives unfolds.
By practicing aparigraha (non-possessiveness), the practitioner lets go of the attachment to material things and the desire to accumulate. This creates mental clarity and freedom, allowing deeper insights into the self. As attachment fades, the practitioner begins to recall knowledge from past lives, gaining an understanding of karmic influences and patterns.

2.40 Through purity, one develops distaste for one's own body and becomes disinterested in contact with others.
Shaucha (purity) leads to an awareness of the physical body as temporary and subject to decay. This realization diminishes attachment to the body and bodily desires. The practitioner becomes more focused on the inner self and less interested in superficial interactions or physical indulgence. This is not a rejection of the body but an understanding that it is only a vehicle for the soul's journey.

2.41 Purity of mind leads to cheerfulness, concentration, control of the senses, and fitness for self-realization.
When the mind is purified through regular practice of purity, the practitioner experiences sattva (clarity and lightness). This leads to a cheerful disposition, increased ability to concentrate, control over the senses, and readiness for deeper meditation and self-realization. Purity aligns the mind and body toward the goal of liberation.

2.42 Contentment brings supreme happiness.
Santosha (contentment) teaches that true happiness doesn't come from external circumstances but from an inner state of acceptance and peace. When the practitioner cultivates contentment, they experience deep, lasting joy regardless of life's ups and downs. This state of inner satisfaction opens the door to spiritual growth and fulfillment.

2.43 Through austerity, impurities of body and senses are destroyed, and perfection in the body and senses is gained.
Tapas (austerity) refers to disciplined, voluntary practices that generate inner heat and purify the body and mind. By engaging in tapas, the practitioner eliminates physical and mental impurities, strengthening both the body and senses. This purification prepares the practitioner for higher levels of meditation and spiritual practice.

2.44 Through self-study, union with the desired deity is achieved.
Svadhyaya (self-study) involves studying sacred texts and reflecting on one's thoughts, habits, and actions. As the practitioner engages in this introspective practice, they deepen their understanding of themselves and their connection to the divine. This ultimately leads to communion with the chosen deity or higher power, creating a bridge between the individual soul and the universal consciousness.

2.45 By surrendering to God, Samadhi is attained.
Ishvara Pranidhana (surrender to God) involves letting go of ego and control, trusting that a higher power is guiding the process of life. This surrender releases the practitioner from the need to achieve results through personal effort alone. By aligning with divine will, the practitioner enters deeper states of concentration and meditation, ultimately reaching Samadhi—the state of union with the self.

2.46 Asana (posture) should be steady and comfortable.
Asana, the physical posture, is one of the eight limbs of yoga. In this sutra, Patanjali emphasizes that the posture should be steady and comfortable, creating a stable foundation for meditation. The goal is not complex physical poses but a posture that allows the body to be still, relaxed, and free from discomfort, so the mind can focus inward.

2.47 This is attained by relaxing effort and meditating on the infinite.
Patanjali teaches that effort in asana should be balanced with relaxation. Rather than forcing the body into a pose, the practitioner should find a place of ease within the posture, letting go of tension and aligning the body with the breath. By meditating on the infinite, or a higher spiritual focus, the practitioner transcends physical limitations and enters a state of deep inner calm.

2.48 Thereafter, one is undisturbed by the dualities of life.
Once the practitioner has mastered a steady and comfortable asana, they become unaffected by the dualities of life—such as heat and cold, pleasure and pain, success and failure. This equanimity is essential for progressing on the path of yoga, as it allows the practitioner to remain calm and focused regardless of external circumstances.

2.49 Pranayama is the regulation of the incoming and outgoing breath after the attainment of asana.
Pranayama, or breath control, follows the mastery of asana. Once the body is steady and comfortable, the practitioner turns their attention to regulating the breath. Pranayama involves controlling the flow of breath in various ways to calm the mind, purify the body, and prepare for deeper states of meditation.

2.50 It consists of external, internal, and restrained breath, observed according to place, time, and number, with breath becoming long and subtle.
Patanjali describes pranayama in detail, explaining that it involves the control of the breath in three stages:
- External (bahya): The exhalation phase.
- Internal (abhyantara): The inhalation phase.
- Restrained (stambha): The retention or holding of the breath.

By practicing pranayama with awareness of place, time, and number of breaths, the practitioner gradually extends the breath, making it more subtle and controlled. This practice steadies the mind and body.

2.51 The fourth type of pranayama transcends the external and internal phases.
Beyond the regulation of the breath in the traditional stages of inhalation, exhalation, and retention, there is a fourth type of pranayama that transcends the need for these distinctions. This is a state where the breath becomes effortless and natural, leading to a deep state of meditation and inner stillness.

2.52 Through pranayama, the veil over the inner light is destroyed.
Pranayama helps clear the mind of distractions and impurities, removing the veil that obscures the inner light of wisdom and self-realization. By purifying the body and mind, the practice of breath control brings the practitioner closer to their true nature and allows the inner light to shine through.

2.53 And the mind becomes fit for concentration.
As the mind becomes purified and still through pranayama, it becomes more focused and ready for the higher stages of yoga, such as concentration (dharana) and meditation (dhyana). The practitioner gains control over the restless mind and develops the ability to concentrate on a single point for extended periods.

2.54 Pratyahara is the withdrawal of the senses from their objects, such that the senses follow the nature of the mind.
Pratyahara is the fifth limb of yoga and involves the withdrawal of the senses from external stimuli. Instead of being constantly drawn outward by sensory impressions, the senses become controlled and directed inward by the mind. This withdrawal prepares the practitioner for deeper levels of meditation, as distractions from the outside world no longer disturb the mind.

2.55 From this comes the highest mastery over the senses.
When pratyahara is practiced consistently, the practitioner gains complete mastery over the senses. The senses no longer control the mind, and the yogi becomes unaffected by sensory pleasures or pains. This mastery is crucial for achieving deeper levels of concentration and eventually, Samadhi.

BOOK 2 SUMMARY

Sadhana Pada, the second chapter of The Yoga Sutras of Patanjali, delves into the practices and disciplines essential for personal growth and self-mastery. It provides practical guidance for overcoming the barriers that prevent individuals from realizing their true nature.

This chapter begins by introducing Kriya Yoga, which comprises three key practices: tapas (self-discipline), svadhyaya (self-study), and Ishvara pranidhana (surrender to a higher power). These practices aim to purify the mind and body, allowing for deeper spiritual understanding.

Following this, the text discusses the five kleshas, or mental afflictions, which include ignorance, egoism, attachment, aversion, and fear of death. According to Patanjali, these kleshas are the fundamental causes of human suffering, and through yoga, one can overcome them.

A prominent aspect of Sadhana Pada is the presentation of the Eightfold Path (Ashtanga Yoga), a step-by-step guide to spiritual growth. The Eightfold Path consists of yamas (ethical restraints), niyamas (personal observances), asana (physical postures), pranayama (breath control), pratyahara (sense withdrawal), dharana (concentration), dhyana (meditation), and samadhi (enlightenment). Each stage builds upon the previous one, leading practitioners toward elevated consciousness and, ultimately, liberation.

Sadhana Pada offers a thorough guide for those dedicated to the spiritual journey, highlighting the importance of self-discipline, ethical behavior, and the progressive refinement of the body, mind, and spirit.

3 VIBHUTI PADA (BOOK ON ACCOMPLISHMENTS)

INTRODUCTION TO BOOK 3

Book 3 of The Yoga Sutras of Patanjali, known as Vibhuti Pada, explores the advanced stages of yogic practice and the extraordinary powers, or siddhis, that arise from deep concentration, meditation, and Samadhi. The term "Vibhuti" refers to these powers, which are not supernatural in essence but the natural outcome of mastering the mind and focusing on specific objects or concepts through the practice of Samyama—a combination of dharana (concentration), dhyana (meditation), and Samadhi (complete absorption).

While the powers described in this chapter—such as knowledge of the past and future, telepathy, levitation, and control over the elements—may seem remarkable, Patanjali cautions that they are not the ultimate goal of yoga. Instead, these abilities serve as milestones on the path to Kaivalya, or liberation, and should not become distractions. The true aim of yoga remains the realization of the self as pure consciousness, free from the constraints of the body, mind, and material world.

Patanjali emphasizes that the yogi must remain detached from these powers to avoid being led astray by pride or ego. The chapter also provides insight into the nature of transformation—both in the mind and in the external world—explaining that through the mastery of Samyama, the practitioner gains a deeper understanding of time, space, and the elements. Ultimately, Vibhuti Pada highlights the importance of balance: while siddhis reflect the advanced capabilities of the mind, they must be transcended to achieve the ultimate goal of self-realization and liberation.

This chapter serves as a guide for practitioners who are reaching higher levels of yoga, offering both an exploration of the powers that can manifest and a reminder that true mastery lies in remaining focused on the pursuit of enlightenment.

BOOK 3

3.1 Concentration (dharana) is the binding of the mind to one place, object, or idea.
Patanjali begins by introducing dharana, the first step of Samyama. Concentration involves fixing the mind on a single point or object, whether external or internal. This focused attention helps the practitioner control the natural tendency of the mind to wander and lays the foundation for deeper meditative states. Dharana can be practiced on various objects such as the breath, a mantra, or even the heart.

3.2 Meditation (dhyana) is the continuous flow of the mind toward that object.
The second component of Samyama is dhyana or meditation. Meditation is an uninterrupted flow of concentration, where the mind remains steadily focused on the chosen object without distraction. Unlike dharana, where effort is required to bring the mind back to the point of focus, dhyana is more effortless and fluid, allowing the practitioner to stay absorbed in the object for extended periods.

3.3 When the mind becomes absorbed in the object alone, free from any self-awareness, this is Samadhi.
Samadhi, the third component of Samyama, is the state of complete absorption. In Samadhi, the practitioner becomes one with the object of meditation, with no distinction between the observer and the observed. Self-awareness dissolves, and only the object remains in the mind. This state of oneness is essential for achieving higher knowledge and insights, as it allows the practitioner to transcend the dualities of perception.

3.4 The combination of these three practices—concentration, meditation, and Samadhi—is called samyama.
Samyama is the simultaneous application of dharana (concentration), dhyana (meditation), and Samadhi (absorption). It is the key to unlocking extraordinary knowledge and powers. When the practitioner masters Samyama, they gain control over the mind and can direct it toward any object or concept to gain deep insight or abilities.

3.5 By mastering samyama, the light of higher knowledge is attained.
Through the practice of Samyama, the practitioner gains access to prajna loka, or the light of higher knowledge. This knowledge is not ordinary intellectual understanding but an intuitive, direct perception of the truth. It allows the yogi to see beyond appearances and comprehend the deeper workings of reality.

3.6 This practice is to be applied in stages.
Patanjali emphasizes that Samyama is not an instantaneous process. Mastery comes gradually as the practitioner applies it step by step to various objects and concepts. The abilities and knowledge attained through Samyama evolve progressively as one deepens their practice and understanding.

3.7 These three (dharana, dhyana, and Samadhi) are more internal compared to the earlier stages of yoga.
In this sutra, Patanjali distinguishes the higher limbs of yoga (dharana, dhyana, and Samadhi) from the earlier limbs (yama, niyama, asana, pranayama, and pratyahara). The earlier stages focus on external discipline and preparation, while Samyama is internal and involves deep control of the mind. These internal practices are considered more advanced and lead directly to self-realization.

3.8 Even these are external compared to nirbija Samadhi (Samadhi without seed).
Although the practice of Samyama is internal and advanced, Patanjali notes that it is still external compared to nirbija Samadhi, the highest state of consciousness where the mind is completely free from any object of focus (the "seed"). Nirbija Samadhi is the state of ultimate liberation, where even the impressions of the mind are transcended.

3.9 The transformation of the mind from distraction to stillness, with the impressions of stillness becoming dominant, is called nirodha parinama (the transformation of cessation).
Nirodha parinama refers to the mental transformation where the tendency toward distraction is replaced by stillness. In this state, the impressions of stillness overpower the usual restlessness of the mind. This transformation is the result of sustained practice and is a crucial step toward Samadhi.

3.10 This state of the mind, with the flow of tranquility, leads to the establishment of inner calm through the force of the latent impressions of stillness.
In this sutra, Patanjali explains that once the mind has experienced stillness, the latent impressions (samskaras) of that stillness begin to dominate, allowing the mind to remain calm even in challenging situations. This inner calm is the foundation of deeper meditative states.

3.11 When the mind becomes one-pointed, as distractions decrease and focus increases, this is called Samadhi parinama (the transformation of Samadhi).
Samadhi parinama occurs when the mind becomes fully concentrated on one object, and distractions are eliminated. The practitioner moves from a state of fluctuating awareness to one-pointed focus, marking the progression toward complete absorption (Samadhi). This transformation signifies that the mind is ready for deeper insights.

3.12 When the mind moves between states of stillness and activity, with the ability to focus equally on both, this is called ekagrata parinama (the transformation of one-pointedness).
In ekagrata parinama, the mind achieves mastery over both stillness and activity. The practitioner is able to maintain one-pointed concentration even when the mind transitions between different states. This ability to stay focused under varying conditions is key to maintaining control over the mind and attaining higher knowledge.

3.13 Through this, the changes in the characteristics, qualities, and conditions of the elements and senses are explained.
Patanjali shifts to explaining how mastery over the mind leads to understanding the transformations in the external world, including the elements and the senses. By controlling the mind, the yogi gains insight into how changes in the material world occur and can influence or transcend them.

3.14 The substratum of these transformations is the ever-changing characteristics, which may be past, present, or future.
All objects in the material world are subject to change, and these changes are based on the underlying characteristics of the objects. These characteristics can manifest in the past, present, or future. Understanding this dynamic helps the practitioner grasp the nature of reality and how transformations occur over time.

3.15 The cause of the difference in these transformations is the sequence of changes.
Patanjali notes that the sequence in which transformations occur is what causes differences in the external world. By understanding the sequence of changes, the practitioner can predict future transformations and gain mastery over the material world.

3.16 By practicing samyama on the three kinds of transformations, knowledge of past and future is attained.
When the yogi practices Samyama on the transformations of objects (their characteristics, qualities, and conditions), they gain knowledge of both the past and future. This siddhi (power) allows the practitioner to perceive the full timeline of an object or person, from its origin to its final state.

3.17 By practicing samyama on the relationship between word, meaning, and object, the knowledge of the sounds of all beings is attained.
Language is a complex interplay between sound (word), its meaning, and the object it refers to. By mastering Samyama on this relationship, the practitioner can understand the sounds and languages of all beings, including animals, and even hear unspoken thoughts.

3.18 By practicing samyama on impressions and their causes, knowledge of past lives is attained.
Our actions and experiences leave impressions (samskaras) on the mind. By practicing Samyama on these impressions, the yogi gains insight into their past lives, understanding the causes and effects that have shaped their present existence.

3.19 By practicing samyama on the mind of another, knowledge of that person's thoughts is attained.
Through Samyama on the mind of another person, the practitioner can directly perceive their thoughts. This is a significant power that demonstrates the deep connection between minds once mental barriers are dissolved.

3.20 However, this does not reveal the specific content of those thoughts, as they are not an object of that practice.
Though the practitioner can perceive the general mental state of another person, the specific content of the thoughts (such as words or detailed ideas) remains hidden unless further Samyama is applied.

3.21 By practicing samyama on the form of the body, the power to make the body invisible by preventing light from contacting the eyes is attained.

Samyama on the body's form allows the yogi to manipulate the perception of others. By controlling the interaction of light with the body, the practitioner can make themselves invisible, not through disappearance, but by disrupting others' ability to see them.

3.22 By practicing samyama on karma, knowledge of one's impending death is attained.

By understanding the workings of karma through Samyama, the practitioner can perceive the timing of their death. This siddhi provides insight into the karmic forces that shape life and death, allowing the yogi to anticipate and prepare for significant life events.

3.23 By practicing samyama on friendliness and other virtues, great strength is attained.

Samyama can also be used to cultivate inner virtues such as friendliness, compassion, and kindness. By deepening these qualities, the practitioner gains spiritual strength, which attracts support from others and brings inner harmony.

3.24 By practicing samyama on the strength of an elephant, the power of an elephant is attained.

This sutra highlights that by practicing samyama on the strength of an elephant, a yogi can tap into that specific power and embody similar strength. This is an example of how the focused mind can draw on the characteristics of an object or being and manifest them in the practitioner's own life.

3.25 By practicing samyama on subtle perceptions, knowledge of hidden or distant things is attained.
By focusing on subtlety in perception, the yogi can understand things that are hidden from the ordinary senses, whether these things are distant or unseen. This siddhi provides an extraordinary ability to perceive beyond physical limitations, offering the yogi profound insights into matters that are normally beyond human perception.

3.26 By practicing samyama on the sun, knowledge of the planetary systems is attained.
The sun represents the center of our solar system, and by practicing samyama on it, the yogi can gain deep knowledge of planetary systems and the cosmic order. This siddhi reflects the yogi's ability to tune into the vastness of the universe and comprehend its functioning on a grand scale.

3.27 By practicing samyama on the moon, knowledge of the positions of the stars is attained.
The moon, being closely linked to the movement of the stars and the night sky, can serve as a focal point for samyama. Through meditation on the moon, the practitioner can gain detailed knowledge of the positions and movements of the stars, enhancing their understanding of the cosmic order.

3.28 By practicing samyama on the pole star, knowledge of the movement of the stars is attained.
The pole star is a fixed point in the sky, often used as a navigational reference. Through samyama on this star, the yogi can acquire precise knowledge of the movements of the stars and the celestial cycles, which can assist in understanding time and cosmic rhythms.

3.29 By practicing samyama on the navel, knowledge of the structure of the body is attained.
The navel is considered a center of life energy in the body, often associated with vitality and the core of the human form. By focusing on the navel in samyama, the practitioner gains insight into the structure and functioning of their own body, including its energetic systems and physical anatomy.

3.30 By practicing samyama on the throat, hunger and thirst are overcome.
Focusing on the throat area in samyama allows the yogi to control sensations of hunger and thirst. This practice provides mastery over bodily needs, helping the yogi maintain focus on higher spiritual pursuits without being distracted by physical desires or discomforts.

3.31 By practicing samyama on the tortoise nerve (kurma nadi), stability of the body is attained.
The kurma nadi is a subtle nerve associated with balance and stability. By focusing on this nerve, the practitioner attains physical and mental steadiness, making the body and mind resilient against external disturbances and allowing for deeper meditation.

3.32 By practicing samyama on the light at the top of the head, visions of perfected beings are attained.
This refers to the crown chakra or the energy center at the top of the head, often associated with spiritual awakening and enlightenment. By concentrating on this area, the practitioner may experience visions of divine or enlightened beings, offering spiritual guidance and inspiration.

3.33 Through intuitive knowledge, everything is known.
This siddhi refers to pratibha, the intuitive flash of knowledge that transcends logical reasoning. Through the development of intuition, the practitioner gains access to all forms of knowledge, both material and spiritual, without the need for external study or inquiry.

3.34 By practicing samyama on the heart, knowledge of the mind is attained.
The heart is considered the seat of consciousness and the true self. By practicing samyama on the heart, the practitioner gains deep insight into the workings of their own mind, as well as the minds of others. This allows for an understanding of thoughts, emotions, and intentions at a profound level.

3.35 The distinction between the pure self and the intellect allows one to experience the true nature of the soul, separate from the body and mind.
By discriminating between the purusha (the pure self) and the buddhi (the intellect), the practitioner experiences the separation between the eternal, unchanging self and the temporary, changing mind. This distinction is crucial for attaining liberation, as it frees the individual from identification with the material world and the mind.

3.36 From this realization arise supernatural hearing, touch, sight, taste, and smell.
When the practitioner fully realizes the difference between the self and the mind, the senses are no longer limited by the body. The yogi attains divya (supernatural) sensory abilities, enabling them to perceive sounds, sights, tastes, smells, and touches that are beyond ordinary human capacity.

3.37 These powers, however, are obstacles to Samadhi when the mind is distracted by their allure.
While these powers may seem impressive, Patanjali warns that they can become distractions on the path to liberation. If the practitioner becomes attached to or distracted by these siddhis, it hinders their progress toward the ultimate goal of Samadhi and Kaivalya (liberation).

3.38 By practicing samyama on the separation of the mind from the body, the practitioner can enter another body.
This extraordinary siddhi enables the yogi to temporarily leave their own body and enter another, gaining control over that body. While remarkable, Patanjali once again advises against becoming fascinated with these abilities, as they are secondary to the goal of self-realization.

3.39 By mastering the life-force (udana), the practitioner can rise above water, mud, thorns, and achieve freedom at the time of death.
Mastery of the udana life-force allows the practitioner to transcend physical limitations. They can move freely through water, mud, or other obstacles, and at the time of death, this control over the life-force allows for a conscious and peaceful departure from the body.

3.40 By mastering the equalizing life-force (samana), the practitioner radiates inner fire.
The samana life-force governs digestion and the distribution of energy within the body. By mastering this force, the practitioner is able to generate inner heat, which can be used for healing, purification, and increased vitality.

3.41 By practicing samyama on the relationship between hearing and space, divine hearing is attained.
This siddhi enables the practitioner to hear sounds from great distances or beyond the physical range of hearing. The yogi can tune into subtle sounds in space, gaining access to knowledge that would otherwise be inaccessible.

3.42 By practicing samyama on the relationship between the body and space, the ability to move through space is attained.
Through mastery of this practice, the yogi can transcend the physical limitations of the body and move freely through space. This siddhi allows for levitation or the ability to travel over great distances in a manner beyond ordinary physical movement.

3.43 When the mind is free from the need to interact with the physical body, the light of pure consciousness shines.
When the practitioner becomes detached from the physical body and no longer identifies with it, the light of pure consciousness (purusha) shines through. This light represents the practitioner's true self, beyond the physical form and material attachments.

3.44 By practicing samyama on the elements—gross, subtle, and causal—the mastery of the elements is attained.
By practicing samyama on the five elements—earth, water, fire, air, and ether—the yogi gains mastery over them. This includes control over their gross (physical), subtle (energetic), and causal (fundamental) aspects, allowing the yogi to manipulate the elements in extraordinary ways.

3.45 This mastery leads to abilities like becoming small, light, and impervious, and to perfection in the body.
Mastery over the elements bestows the practitioner with the ability to alter the body's properties, such as becoming extremely small (anima), light (laghima), or impervious to harm. It also leads to the perfection of the body, where it becomes strong, resilient, and invulnerable to physical dangers.

3.46 Perfection in the body includes beauty, grace, strength, and invulnerability.
As the practitioner continues to develop mastery over the body through yoga, it becomes a perfect vessel for spiritual practice. This perfection manifests as beauty, physical grace, strength, and an invulnerability that protects the body from harm or decay.

3.47 By practicing samyama on the relationship between the senses and their objects, mastery over the senses is attained.
The senses are typically drawn outward to the objects of desire, but through samyama, the yogi gains control over this tendency. By mastering the relationship between the senses and their objects, the practitioner becomes free from sensory attachments and can direct the senses inward toward self-realization.

3.48 This leads to swiftness of mind, freedom from sensory limitations, and mastery over the natural world.
When the senses are mastered, the mind becomes swift and agile, capable of moving quickly from one thought or object to another. The yogi also transcends sensory limitations, gaining freedom from the constraints of time, space, and the material world. This mastery extends to controlling natural phenomena, demonstrating the deep connection between the mind and the elements.

3.49 With the realization of the difference between the pure self and the intellect, mastery over all states of existence and omniscience is attained.
When the yogi fully realizes the distinction between the purusha (pure self) and the intellect (buddhi), they attain mastery over all states of existence. This realization brings sarvajnatva (omniscience), where the practitioner gains complete knowledge of the universe and its workings.

3.50 Through non-attachment to even these powers, the seeds of ignorance are destroyed, and liberation (Kaivalya) is attained.
Despite the attainment of these extraordinary powers, Patanjali stresses that the yogi must remain detached from them. Only through non-attachment to these siddhis can the practitioner destroy the seeds of ignorance (avidya) and achieve Kaivalya—liberation from the cycle of birth and death.

3.51 Invitations from heavenly beings should be disregarded to avoid pride and distraction, which would lead to undesirable outcomes.
As the yogi progresses in their practice, they may receive invitations or distractions from divine beings or celestial realms. However, Patanjali warns against indulging in these temptations, as they can lead to pride and divert the practitioner from the ultimate goal of liberation.

3.52 By practicing samyama on the moments and their sequence, knowledge born of discrimination is attained.
By focusing on the nature of time and its sequence of moments, the practitioner develops viveka jnana (knowledge born of discrimination). This knowledge enables the yogi to distinguish between subtle differences in objects, events, and moments, allowing for a clear perception of reality.

3.53 This discriminative knowledge allows the practitioner to distinguish between things that appear identical based on their characteristics, place, and time.
With viveka jnana, the practitioner can perceive even the smallest distinctions between things that may appear identical to others. This ability to differentiate is crucial for understanding the true nature of reality and overcoming delusions of the mind.

3.54 This knowledge, born of discrimination, transcends all objects and forms of knowledge, leading to omniscience.
The knowledge that arises from viveka jnana is not limited to any particular object or field; it transcends all forms of knowledge, giving the practitioner access to sarvajnatva (omniscience). This omniscience allows the yogi to understand all things, past, present, and future.

3.55 When the purity of the intellect equals the purity of the self, liberation (Kaivalya) is attained.
The final stage of the yogic path is reached when the purity of the intellect matches the purity of the self. At this point, all mental impurities and distractions have been removed, and the practitioner experiences Kaivalya, the ultimate state of liberation, where the self is free from all attachments and limitations.

BOOK 3 SUMMARY

Vibhuti Pada is the third chapter of The Yoga Sutras of Patanjali, focusing on the extraordinary powers, or "vibhutis," that arise from deep meditation and spiritual practice. This chapter emphasizes the importance of concentration, meditation, and absorption, collectively known as Samyama, as the means to unlock these powers.

The chapter begins by outlining the three stages of mental discipline: dharana (concentration), dhyana (meditation), and samadhi (absorption). When practiced together as Samyama, they lead to heightened awareness and the development of various siddhis, or supernormal abilities. These abilities can include things like telepathy, invisibility, and knowledge of past lives.

However, Patanjali warns that these powers, while impressive, can also become distractions from the ultimate goal of spiritual liberation. The true aim of yoga is not to gain supernatural abilities but to transcend the ego and achieve freedom from suffering.

Vibhuti Pada also explores the idea that by mastering these inner states, practitioners can go beyond ordinary limitations of the mind and body. Yet, the text stresses that the practitioner must remain focused on the higher spiritual path, using these abilities as tools for greater self-awareness rather than as ends in themselves.

In essence, Vibhuti Pada teaches that while spiritual powers are possible, they should not divert the yogi from the ultimate goal of self-realization and liberation.

4 KAIVALYA PADA (BOOK ON ABSOLUTENESS)

INTRODUCTION TO BOOK 4

Book 4 of The Yoga Sutras of Patanjali, known as Kaivalya Pada, focuses on the ultimate goal of yoga: Kaivalya, or liberation. This chapter outlines the final stages of the yogic journey, where the practitioner transcends the material world, mental fluctuations, and the cycle of karma to achieve a state of absolute independence.

Patanjali begins by explaining how extraordinary powers (siddhis) can manifest through different methods, such as birth, herbs, mantras, austerities, and Samadhi. However, these powers are not the goal of yoga. Instead, Patanjali emphasizes that the true purpose of yoga is to free oneself from the influence of the gunas (the three fundamental qualities of nature: sattva, rajas, and tamas), which drive the cycles of birth and death, pleasure and pain, and attachment and aversion.

As the practitioner progresses, they realize the distinction between the mind and the purusha (pure consciousness). Through the practice of discrimination and self-awareness, the yogi detaches from the mind's activities and identifies with the purusha, leading to the dissolution of karmic seeds and the elimination of mental afflictions. Once the gunas cease to influence the purusha, the self-rests in its true, unchanging nature.

This chapter highlights that liberation is not the attainment of powers but the realization of the purusha as pure consciousness, free from the material world. Kaivalya, the state of absolute freedom, is the final destination of the yogic path, where the self exists beyond the constraints of time, space, and the body, experiencing eternal peace and independence. The Kaivalya Pada serves as a profound guide for those seeking the ultimate liberation from the cycles of existence and the discovery of their true self.

4.1 The powers (siddhis) are produced by birth, herbs, mantra, austerities, or Samadhi.

Patanjali begins by explaining the various ways in which extraordinary powers (siddhis) can manifest. These powers may arise naturally at birth, through the use of certain medicinal herbs, through the repetition of mantras, through intense austerities, or through the practice of Samadhi (deep meditation). While these powers are remarkable, Patanjali warns that they are not the goal of yoga and should not distract the practitioner from the pursuit of liberation.

4.2 The transformation into another type of birth results from the overflow of nature's latent tendencies.

Here, Patanjali refers to the process of parinama (transformation), where latent tendencies in the mind and body manifest into different forms or even new lifetimes. The fundamental nature of the individual remains constant, but the expressions of their characteristics change as they evolve spiritually. This transformation is part of the journey toward liberation, as the yogi gradually sheds attachments and impurities.

4.3 The instrumental cause does not directly produce transformation in nature's powers; it merely removes obstacles, like a farmer clearing a channel for water.

In this sutra, Patanjali emphasizes that the practice of yoga does not directly create liberation but rather removes the obstacles that block it. Just as a farmer does not create water but simply clears a channel for it to flow, the yogi's practice removes the impurities that obstruct the natural state of liberation. The innate power of consciousness is always present, and yoga helps clear the way for its full expression.

4.4 Consciousness is created only from the sense of individuality (asmita).

The sense of asmita (individuality or ego) creates the false identification of the self with the mind, body, and personality. This limited consciousness is what gives rise to the idea of a separate self. However, the true self, purusha, is beyond individuality, and realizing this distinction is key to achieving liberation.

4.5 Although the activities of different minds may vary, one mind is the director of all those minds.
While individual minds may experience different thoughts and activities, they are all ultimately governed by a single consciousness—purusha. The mind is merely an instrument for experiencing the world, but the true source of perception and awareness is the pure, unchanging self.

4.6 Of these minds, the one born of meditation is free from latent impressions.
A mind that has been purified through meditation is free from samskaras (latent impressions), which are the residual effects of past actions and experiences. Through continuous meditation, the mind becomes clear and is no longer influenced by past conditioning, allowing the practitioner to experience reality as it is.

4.7 The actions of a yogi are neither white (good) nor black (bad), but for others, they are of three kinds: white, black, or mixed.
For an enlightened yogi, actions no longer generate karma, as they are performed without attachment or desire. Therefore, their actions are neither good nor bad—they are neutral. However, for those who have not yet attained liberation, actions fall into three categories: white (good karma), black (bad karma), or mixed (a combination of both), and these continue to bind them to the cycle of birth and death.

4.8 From these three kinds of karma, only those which correspond to the impressions are manifested.
The karma that manifests in a person's life is directly related to the samskaras (latent impressions) stored in their mind. These impressions determine which actions from past lives come to fruition in the present. The yogi works to eliminate these impressions through practice, thereby transcending the effects of karma.

4.9 Despite the separation of time, the connection between memory and latent impressions remains, as they are similar in nature.
Time does not break the connection between memory and samskaras. Even though experiences from past lives may seem distant, the latent impressions they leave on the mind persist and influence the present life. This continuity explains why certain tendencies or habits persist across lifetimes.

4.10 The latent impressions have no beginning because desire is eternal.
The samskaras that shape our experiences and actions are without beginning because desire itself is eternal. Desire drives the cycle of karma, and as long as desire exists, these latent impressions will continue to shape our lives and bind us to the cycle of birth and death.

4.11 They are maintained by cause, effect, basis, and support. When these are removed, the latent impressions are also removed.
The continuation of samskaras is sustained by the interplay of cause, effect, and the support they receive from the mind and body. When the yogi removes these sustaining factors through practice and detachment, the impressions dissolve, leading to liberation.

4.12 The past and future exist in their own forms. They differ in the manifestation of the characteristics of time.
Patanjali explains that the past, present, and future all exist, but they manifest differently due to the characteristics of time. The future is unmanifested potential, the present is manifesting, and the past is already manifested. This understanding helps the practitioner perceive time as a continuum rather than as separate events.

4.13 They are either manifest or subtle, and they are composed of the three gunas.
All things—whether manifest or subtle—are composed of the three gunas (qualities): sattva (purity), rajas (activity), and tamas (inertia). These gunas constantly interact to create the physical and mental experiences of life, but the enlightened yogi sees beyond these qualities to recognize the true nature of the self.

4.14 The essence of an object remains constant, whether the form appears to change due to transformations in the gunas.
Even though an object may change its appearance or characteristics due to the shifting balance of the gunas, its essence remains constant. This is a key insight for the yogi, who learns to look beyond external transformations and recognize the unchanging reality beneath them.

4.15 The same object is perceived differently by different minds.
Each person's perception of an object is shaped by their unique mind, experiences, and latent impressions. Thus, the same object can be perceived in many different ways. This highlights the subjectivity of perception and underscores the importance of transcending the mind to see reality as it is.

4.16 An object does not depend on a single mind for its existence. Otherwise, what would happen to it when not perceived?
Patanjali asserts that objects exist independently of individual perception. The existence of an object is not contingent upon being perceived by a specific mind, as it would continue to exist even when no one is observing it. This reinforces the objective reality of the material world.

4.17 The object is known or unknown depending on whether the mind is colored by it.
Whether or not the mind perceives an object depends on whether it is "colored" or influenced by the object. When the mind is focused on or impacted by an object, it becomes aware of it. Otherwise, the object remains unknown or unnoticed.

4.18 The modifications of the mind are always known to the purusha (the pure self) because the purusha is unchanging.
The purusha, or pure consciousness, is always aware of the fluctuations and modifications of the mind. While the mind changes and interacts with the world, the purusha remains a constant, unchanging witness to these activities.

4.19 The mind is not self-illuminating because it is an object of perception, just like external objects.
Patanjali explains that the mind itself is not self-aware or self-illuminating. It is an object of perception, much like other external objects, and requires the purusha (the true self) to observe it and give it awareness.

4.20 The mind cannot perceive both itself and another object at the same time.
The mind cannot simultaneously focus on itself and an external object. This limitation of the mind demonstrates the need to transcend its functions in order to experience the purusha, which is beyond duality and simultaneous perception.

4.21 If one mind were to perceive another mind, an infinite regress would result, along with confusion of memory.
If one mind attempted to perceive another, this would lead to an endless loop of perception, causing confusion and mixing of memories. Patanjali uses this to illustrate the limitations of the mind and the need to focus inwardly toward the purusha.

4.22 When the mind is colored by both the seer and the seen, it appears to comprehend everything.
The mind, when influenced by both the seer (purusha) and the seen (external objects), can give the illusion of comprehending everything. However, this comprehension is incomplete, as it is still influenced by duality and not the true realization of the self.

4.23 The mind, though colored by countless latent impressions, exists for another's purpose (purusha) because it acts in conjunction with others.
The mind, despite being influenced by numerous samskaras, ultimately exists to serve the purusha. It acts as an instrument for experience and perception, but its purpose is to assist in the journey toward self-realization and liberation.

4.24 For one who has realized the distinction between purusha and the mind, there is no further identification with the mind's activity.
Once the yogi has realized the difference between the purusha and the mind, they no longer identify with the mind's thoughts, emotions, or actions. This disidentification is crucial for attaining liberation, as the yogi recognizes that the mind is merely a tool and not the true self.

4.25 When discrimination becomes perfect, the mind inclines toward liberation.
When the yogi's discriminative knowledge becomes complete, the mind naturally moves toward liberation. This occurs when the practitioner consistently distinguishes between the real (purusha) and the unreal (mind and external world), allowing them to break free from ignorance and attachment.

4.26 When there are breaks in this discrimination, other thoughts arise due to residual impressions.
Even after gaining discriminative knowledge, residual samskaras can cause distractions and interruptions in the yogi's practice. These latent impressions can trigger thoughts and emotions that temporarily pull the practitioner away from their focus on liberation.

4.27 These obstacles are to be overcome in the same manner as the afflictions.
Patanjali advises that the residual impressions that arise should be dealt with in the same way as the kleshas (mental afflictions). Through consistent practice and detachment, the yogi can neutralize these impressions and maintain their progress toward liberation.

4.28 Even for the person uninterested in the fruits of their actions, discriminative knowledge brings about Samadhi, known as dharma-megha (cloud of virtues).
When the yogi has perfected discriminative knowledge and no longer desires the fruits of their actions, they attain a state of dharma-megha Samadhi. This is a state of deep meditation where the practitioner is immersed in virtue and wisdom, free from karmic consequences.

4.29 From this Samadhi, the afflictions and karmic seeds are destroyed.
In dharma-megha Samadhi, the seeds of karma and the mental afflictions are completely eradicated. The yogi is no longer bound by past actions or future consequences, having transcended the cycle of cause and effect.

4.30 Then, all the coverings of ignorance are removed, and infinite knowledge arises.
Once the afflictions and karma are destroyed, the yogi is freed from the coverings of ignorance (avidya). This results in the rise of ananta jnana (infinite knowledge), where the yogi perceives reality in its totality without any distortion or limitation.

4.31 With the removal of ignorance, the gunas (qualities of nature) cease to function for the purusha, and the practitioner attains the final goal of yoga—liberation.
When ignorance is eliminated, the gunas (sattva, rajas, and tamas) no longer exert their influence over the purusha. The practitioner attains Kaivalya—the state of absolute independence and liberation—where the self is free from the forces of nature and rests in its pure, unchanging essence.

4.32 Time, which is the sequence of moments, becomes evident through transformations of nature.
Patanjali explains that time is perceived as the sequence of changes in nature. These transformations create the experience of time, but the yogi who has transcended nature no longer experiences time in the same way, having moved beyond the limitations of past, present, and future.

4.33 Kaivalya (liberation) is the return of the gunas to their original state, no longer serving the purusha, who stands in its own true nature as pure consciousness.

Patanjali describes Kaivalya as the return of the gunas to their original state. The gunas, having fulfilled their purpose, no longer influence the purusha. The purusha rests in its own true nature, free from the cycles of karma, time, and material existence. This is the ultimate state of liberation, where the self-experiences absolute independence and eternal peace.

4.34 Liberation (Kaivalya) is the reversal of the flow of the gunas, which have fulfilled their purpose, and the power of consciousness (purusha) rests in its own nature. This is the state of absolute independence.

In the final sutra of The Yoga Sutras, Patanjali summarizes the culmination of the entire yogic path: Kaivalya, or liberation. Here, the gunas (the qualities of nature—sattva, rajas, and tamas) that have previously driven the processes of life, thought, and karma, recede. Their role is complete because they have helped the practitioner reach the ultimate realization of the self.

BOOK 4 SUMMARY

Kaivalya Pada, the final chapter of The Yoga Sutras of Patanjali, focuses on achieving ultimate liberation, or kaivalya. It discusses the nature of the mind, the influence of karma, and how yoga practice frees the mind from these effects.

Patanjali explains that liberation comes when the practitioner realizes the self, or purusha, is separate from the mind and material world. This realization leads to freedom from suffering and the cycle of rebirth.

The chapter emphasizes detachment from the ego and material attachments, highlighting that true liberation is found through pure awareness and the removal of ignorance, leading to complete independence and spiritual freedom.

www.ingramcontent.com/pod-product-compliance
Ingram Content Group UK Ltd.
Pitfield, Milton Keynes, MK11 3LW, UK
UKHW021410190726
13845UKWH00028B/996

9 789348 535276